LIFT-OFF
TO FAITH

CONTENTS

The photographs in this book are reproduced by permission of the following photographers and organizations:
Associated Press 16-17; Barnaby's Picture Library 12-13, 18-19, 24-25, 32-33 (hang glider); British Airways 6-7; Branse Burbridge 44-45 (Japanese, Mexicans and international students); Camera Press 20-21; Church Missionary Society 8-9 (famine), 44-45 (families in Tanzania and India); Decca Navigational Co Ltd 42-43; Noel Gay Artists Ltd 26-27 (trapeze artists); Alan Hutchinson Library 8-9 (surgeons), 30-31, 56-57 (food bowls); IBM United Kingdom Ltd 8-9 (computer graphics); Lion Publishing: Jon Willcocks 10-11 (tree), 14-15, 46-47 (ripples), 50-51 (potter), 56-57 (banquet) and end papers Mercury Press Agency 60-61 (building); National Youth Orchestra of Great Britain (at Royal Hospital School, Holbrook), by courtesy of sponsors Lloyds Bank—photo by Tony Stone 8-9; Open Doors 44-45 (communion); Popperfoto 22-23 (parachute), 28-29, 32-33 (rocket), 34-35, 36-37, 46-47 (volcano), 52-53, 54-55; Press Association 40-41; South American Missionary Society 44-45 (peasants); Swiss National Tourist Office (Davos) 50-51; Syndication International 22-23 (sky bike); John P. Taylor: Oikoumene 60-61 (children); Topham 10-11 (ship); T. J. Willcocks 8-9 (agriculture); Rev. John Woolmer 58-59 (all); World Vision Picture Library 38-39.

Copyright 1981 Lion Publishing

Published by
Lion Publishing
Icknield Way, Tring, Herts, England
ISBN 0 85648 548 9

Albatross Books
PO Box 320, Sutherland, NSW 2232, Australia
ISBN 0 86760 456 5

First edition 1981
This edition 1985

Printed in Yugoslavia by Mladinska knjiga

LIFT-OFF TO FAITH

MICHAEL GREEN

A LION BOOK
Tring · Belleville · Sydney

FASTEN YOUR SAFETY BELTS

The world in which we live has been shrunk to a 'global village' by modern communications and technology.

The New York businessman leaves John F. Kennedy Airport after breakfast, cruises at twice the speed of sound over the Atlantic, and arrives in London in time for lunch.

But what sort of world is it for most of its inhabitants? Is technology really going to solve the big questions facing humanity today?

Mind-blowing

And how can we understand ourselves —the race who people this planet? On the one hand we achieve scientific miracles. On the other hand we invent sickening cruelties and vices.

Every day television news blows our minds with stories of cruelty, suffering, guerrilla warfare, violence.

Have we really advanced morally from the barbarism of ancient times? *Has Christianity a place in today's world? If technology sidesteps our deeper questions, what sort of answers can we find in the*

Christian faith? Or is it a survival from our pre-scientific past? A superstition we have outgrown?

Western society is now largely secular. It is concerned with this world and unaware of any other. So too, increasingly, are the urban societies of Asia, Africa, Latin America. Many Arab countries are fast moving in the same direction, though it is exactly this development that the Iranian revolution has tried to reverse. In the 'socialist' blocs, religion of any sort is officially scorned or actively persecuted.

Advance

But this is not the whole picture. There is strong evidence that *worldwide* Christianity is in a phase of advance, despite its local decline in the West.

Membership of churches in many third-world countries is growing astonishingly fast. In Uganda, even under Idi Amin's destructive regime, the Christian proportion of the population rose from just over 50 per cent to about 75 per cent. And it has been claimed for the whole of Africa south of the Sahara that if conversions continue at the present rate the whole region will be Christian by the year 2,000.

Fresh air

Many young people across the world are finding that Christianity has something to say to them for the 1980s. It may not fit *comfortably* in the modern world. True Christianity has never been comfortable. But it talks about real issues from a radical standpoint.

In an age of empty slogans and a massive identity crisis, the Christian promise of new life in Christ is felt by many to be a breath of fresh air.

GOD AT WORK

Is life just a confused chaos of human activity, happiness, misery, life, death? Or is there something to it? Is there something going on here that makes sense?

Christians believe that God is at work in the world. He made it in the first place. But he did not simply go away and leave everything to its own devices. Not even a human creator would do that. God is involved in his world. He 'holds it together'.

No one has ever seen God. We may find the signs of his activity in the world hard to spot. But (as the apostle Paul wrote) 'since the creation of the world God's invisible qualities—his eternal power and divine nature—have been clearly seen, being understood from what has been made…'

The plan

God is at work in the world. He is 'general manager' of the whole outfit.

Nothing—not even the dark side of life—happens without God's permission.

This raises many questions. How can a good God allow suffering and evil? There is so much we do not understand...now. But Christians see a greater purpose in God's plan. The final stage of the world will provide a vantage-point from which all today's joy and pain will be seen in their true meaning.

People

Easier to understand is how God is at work through people. In this way he is involved intimately, personally in every part of life.

Creativity in the arts, technical skill in complex processes, the patient care

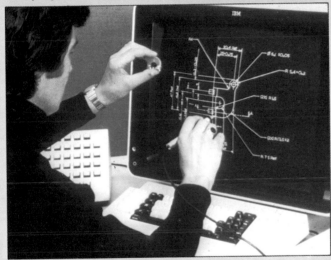

of surgeons in Ethiopia, the practical love shown in famine relief in Bangladesh, the maximizing of earth's resources through 'dry earth' agriculture schemes in Botswana...all these remind us that God is creative, and he carries on creating through the skill he has given us.

To see this gives a boost to developing our creative gifts. It can make our daily job worthwhile.

Resources

Material things are not the whole story. Human resources need developing too. Healing diseased bodies and shattered lives, drawing a parched earth back to productive life...these are things everyone recognizes as good.

Many Christians get involved in such action. But God is equally at work in these ways through many others who do not see their work as his...yet.

AFTER SIN-SICKNESS

Despite all the signs of God at work in the world, it is still in a mess.

● *There is appalling inequality between rich and poor nations. In 1975 the average income in the US was $7,060, in China $350, in India $150.*

● *A massive population explosion is on the way. By the year 2,000 there will be twice as many mouths to feed as there were in 1950. They increase at 210,000 a day — starvation affects more and more of mankind.*

● *The world is running short not only of food but of oil and energy. The age of abundance is over, and yet the West continues in careless extravagance.*

● *The air, the land and the waters of the earth are being ruined. Dumping radioactive waste in the sea is just one of the ways we are poisoning the environment for future generations.*

● *Families are breaking up, with great misery and hurt. One marriage in three collapses.*

● *The crime rate all over the world is accelerating with terrifying rapidity. It is an age of violence and brutality such as the world has never seen. It is the age of concentration camps, of the most exquisite forms of torture, of genocide.*

Evil nature

Leonardo de Vinci suppressed his invention of the submarine, he tells us, 'because of the evil nature of man. They would use it to practice assassinations at the bottom of the sea'. He had put his finger on the heart of our problem: the evil nature of men.

   'What's wrong with the world? I am' said a famous man of letters.

Of course, if you put that to the man in the street he will tell you:

'I've never done anyone any harm.'

'I'm all right.'

'I'm as good as people who go to church.'

Rescue

But Christianity will have none of it. The Christian faith is unashamedly a rescue religion. That is why so many respectable people will have nothing to do with it. The Bible proclaims that we are *not* all right. The world is in a mess, and each individual life is in a mess. 'The heart of man is deceitful above all things and desperately wicked', said the prophet Jeremiah.

Jesus himself tells us something crucial — something that we are painfully having to rediscover today. Will more education or more social welfare put us right? Or is it 'the system'? Change the system and all will be right...

No, said Jesus. It is 'from within, out of the heart of man, that evil thoughts come — theft, murder, deceit, envy, slander, pride, folly.'

Ivy

The fault lies not in our stars but in ourselves. The 'human disease' of self-centredness is nothing short of fatal.

You must have seen a tree throttled by ivy. It is a sad sight. A tree is such a strong, beautiful, living thing. And we feel it ought never to succumb to the insignificant tentacles climbing up it.

But ivy is like a creeping sickness. Look how it starts: so pale, and frail, and innocent-looking. But it grows. It increases its hold, shuts out the light and air, and eventually strangles the life out of the tree.

That is very like the effect on us of the disease the Bible calls sin. We were made to be great — the crown of God's creation. But sin spoils it all. 'Whosoever commits sin becomes a slave of sin,' said Jesus.

'I do not understand my own actions. I do not do what I wish; but what I hate I do... Wretched man that I am! Who shall deliver me?' cried the apostle Paul. 'Sin pays its customers; the wage is death.'

Power to set us free

This is all very unflattering for a generation which thinks it is the greatest. But it is a true analysis, however humiliating. It means that we need two things above all:

● forgiveness for the mess we have made of our world and of our lives;

● and a power beyond our own to set us free.

BATTLE FOR THE MIND

This used to be called the age of the hidden persuaders. The advertisers, TV, films, newspapers—these were the weapons in the battle for the mind.

But the persuaders are no longer hidden. They are strident. Listen to the parrot cries at party political conferences in the West. Listen to the chants of guerrillas in the African bush. Watch the rape of the minds in Russia, China and many other countries. Propaganda...distortion... brainwashing. The battle for the mind is on.

The Roman emperors calculated that if they provided bread and circuses for the masses they could manipulate people very much as they pleased. Today we look to the welfare state for the bread, pop music and football for the circuses, and the result can be much the same. There are plenty of manipulators of the mind in the field today. They are out to produce programmed men.

A faith to live by

Is Christianity just another of the competing, manipulative ideologies in our world? Yet another opiate to dull the pain of daily life? Or does it rightly claim to be true, to be a faith to live by, and a challenge to the manipulators of ideas?

I would want to see these conditions fulfilled in any faith claiming my allegiance for today:

● *It must be true. In the long run men will not be satisfied by a fraud or a lie. Jesus Christ claimed to show the truth about God and man; indeed, to be the truth. Down the ages, his claim has worn well.*

● *It must be relevant. If it makes no difference to the lives of ordinary people, it is no good. It has got to enrich the quality of life. Christianity makes precisely that claim. Jesus said, 'I have come that you may have life, in all its fulness.'*

● *It must be big enough to meet many needs. It must not be petty or individualistic, but wide enough in its scope and influence to transform national and international relationships, to affect medicine, education, ecology, peace and industrial relations. Despite all the failures of churches and individual Christians Jesus Christ has continued to have that effect on the world. Right up to today.*

● *It must have universal appeal. If a faith appeals to one segment of society alone, or one race alone, then it is too small and too narrow for me. But Jesus is the man for all seasons and for all races. He has drawn to himself blacks and whites, rich and poor, clever and simple, Eskimos and Arabs, Communists and capitalists from all over the world. It is happening now, as people all over the world are converted to Christianity at a rate of 60,000 a day. And always his impetus has been towards unity, love and development.*

● *It must be big enough to embrace death. A faith to live by is a poor thing if it is not also a faith to die by. Jesus is the only world leader who claims to have conquered death. Hundreds of millions believe that claim. Because Jesus rose from the grave that first Easter Day, his followers can face death without fear.*

Jesus Christ does not come to us as a hidden persuader or a ruthless dictator. He does not want conformist minds and programmed people. He invites us to consider his claims, to face up to his challenge...and then make a free choice about following him.

WHAT DO WE KNOW ABOUT JESUS?

A century ago there was a lot of talk suggesting that Jesus never existed. 'Just another dying-and-rising god', they said, 'like Greek mythology'. At much the same time Karl Marx was falling under the influence of a theology professor called Bruno Bauer who was sacked for heresy. He maintained that the Jesus story was dreamed up late in the second century. This bizarre view is still official Communist teaching.

Even in the 1970s John Allegro (of magic mushroom fame) was claiming that Jesus was the 'Teacher of Righteousness' of the Dead Sea Scrolls, written about 100 BC. And today there are plenty of people who say he was a visitor from outer space in a UFO.

All such views are doomed to failure. Why? Because they ignore the good historical evidence for Jesus of Nazareth.

● **First, you have the accounts of the life of Jesus, the Gospels, and the letters of the New Testament —** *a completely new literary explosion brought about by Jesus.*

● **Second, there is Roman evidence for Jesus' existence, his unusual birth, his execution by crucifixion under Pontius Pilate, who governed the turbulent province of Judea from 26 to 36 AD (Tacitus, Annals 15.44, Suetonius, Claudius 25, Pliny, Letters 10.95, 96).**

● **Third, there are archaeological remains which show that people**

were worshipping Jesus in Palestine and Italy by the middle of the first century.

● Fourth, Jewish testimony (in Josephus and the Mishnah) makes clear allusions to his unusual birth, his death on the cross, his miracles, his divine claims and the birth of the church. Both Jewish and Roman evidence is hostile to Christians. Therefore its testimony is all the more valuable, and it chimes in closely with what the Gospels tell us.

And what do the Gospels teach? They tell us that Jesus was more than simply the carpenter of Nazareth; more than a famous rabbi; more even than the best of men. But, on the other hand, they never tell us that he was just God Almighty dressed up as a human being.

No, they struggle at the boundaries of language to express their conviction that in Jesus Christ God has shown us what he is like, within the terms of a human life. Not that Jesus was all of God that there is; he constantly spoke of his 'heavenly Father'. Rather, that he

is the tip of the iceberg of God, and the rest of the iceberg is all of a piece with the part we can see.

This is what astounded and thrilled those Jews who became the first Christian believers. Living cheek by jowl with Jesus for three years persuaded them that he was no mere man, but that God himself had cared enough to come and seek us out in the person of Jesus.

If we matter that much to God, no wonder their message became known as 'godspel': good news.

The first recorded words of Jesus electrified his hearers. 'The moment of opportunity has dawned. God's kingdom is at hand. Change your attitudes, and believe the good news!'

The kingdom of God

The kingdom of God featured a great deal in his teaching. He was always talking about it. But what is it?

By 'the kingdom of God' Jesus meant a whole new start for a world gone wrong. Instead of being dominated by selfishness, men would welcome God's rule in their lives. Jesus introduced this kingly rule in a new way; because he, alone of all men, fully obeyed God's will throughout his life. He lived out the kingdom of God whic'

A NEW DIMENSION

he proclaimed. He demonstrated what a life in touch with God at every point would look like.

He was the kingdom in person.

● He showed us what the ideal king is like—perfect, living, challenging, incorruptible.
● He showed us what the ideal subject is like—obedient, full of faith, loyal even up to death.

In other words, if you want to know what God is like, look at Jesus. There you see the perfection of God lived out without distortion in a human life. And if you want to know what people are meant to be like, look at Jesus. There you see in clear focus the full range of human virtues in a life of total dependence on God.

Entering the kingdom

The way to enter this kingdom is very costly, and yet very simple. It means:

● first a total change of priorities and direction, or *repentance*.
● and then trust in and commitment to Jesus Christ, or *faith*.

The way to live in the kingdom is equally costly yet simple. It means saying yes to God's offer to put within us a new life, the life of the kingdom.

The result will be that we begin to try and please him in everything. We get into the habit of asking ourselves, 'How would Jesus have handled this situation?', and acting accordingly. What is more, we begin to discover in experience the power he gives to make that sort of living possible. It is a radically new life.

From fear to love

In recent years the eyes of the world have been on Uganda. The new dimension, the 'kingdom dimension', can be seen very clearly in the terrible situation in which hundreds of thousands of Ugandans, most of them Christian believers, were slaughtered by Idi Amin.

One of these men was Archbishop Janani Luwum, whom I knew well. Gently and firmly he opposed the tyranny of General Amin. Graciously he remonstrated with him, in the name of God and of justice.

When Amin would not listen he had Janani killed.

As he was led to the torture chamber he and another tortured prisoner prayed for the President.

That is the life of the kingdom.

When Amin refused to release the bullet-ridden body, thousands broke a government ban and held a funeral service outside the cathedral in Kampala—with an empty grave. They sang the song of the East African Revival, and the preacher spoke on these words of the New Testament: 'He is not here; he is risen.'

That is the life of the kingdom.

And Janani was not unique. His fellow-bishop, Festo Kivengere, escaped with his life by a hairsbreadth —and then wrote a book called *I love Idi Amin*.

That is the life of the kingdom.

When men live and die like that, the words of Jesus are fulfilled quite literally: 'Blessed are the meek, for they shall inherit the earth.'

That is the life of the kingdom.

FAMILIES NEED FATHERS

In the West two things are happening. Families are breaking up. And the children are getting into trouble.

Absentee fathers lead to delinquency. The family *matters*—and families need fathers.

Much of Jesus' teaching is about God the Father. He said God was his Father. He said God could be our Father.

Like Dad?

And that immediately raises some questions.

'Yes, I believe in God. Something must have started the world off.'

Many people think like that, and it makes sense. But Jesus says that is a very inadequate picture of God. He is a person, not a thing. He is Father. Father in the sense that he gave life to the world and us. Father in the sense that he loves the world and us.

'I can't believe God is like my old man',

people say. Fair enough. Our human fathers often leave much to be desired. The Bible says that all fatherhood derives from God, but it is often a grossly distorted copy. All the same, we have some idea of what a real Father would be like: strong, loving, able to guide and teach and discipline us. Jesus taught that God was like that.

'Yes, but surely we are all sons of God?'

Lots of people assume that. But the Bible says an emphatic 'No' to it—except in the sense that we are all God's creation. You see, sons resemble their fathers. And we do not resemble God. We don't live like him or love like him. Indeed, most of the time we are strangers to him, if not active rebels against him.

Jesus taught that there was only one real Son of God. Himself. He coined a new word for it—'Abba'. It means 'Daddy'. Nobody had ever dared to call God that before Jesus. Nobody had the right to do so.

But Jesus did. He claimed time and again that God was his Abba, his 'dear Father'. In other words, if you wanted to know what the Father was like, you could get a very good idea from the Son. He shared his Father's character, and life, and love.

Sharing the family life

But the really astonishing thing is that this perfect Son of the heavenly Father offers us a share in the family life.

'Jesus came to his own world, and his own people did not receive him.' That is a very fair summary of what happened. But wait… 'However, to those who *did* receive him he gave the right to become sons of God.'

That's what a Christian is: a child of God.

The Christian has his Father to protect, to guide, to give strength. He can enjoy the other members of the Father's family. He loves the Father, wants to please him, delights in being with him and talking to him and thanking him.

You don't become a son of God by the accident of birth.

You don't become a son of God by trying hard to be good.

You don't become a son of God just by being baptized or confirmed.

You become a son of God when you welcome the Son of God into your life.

You then get adopted into God's family. And you never get thrown out. That's what a Christian is, a child of God. It is hardly surprising that crowds flocked to Jesus to hear more.

It is hardly surprising that John, one of Jesus' disciples, burst out: 'See what love the Father has given us that we should be called sons of God. And so we are.'

COSMIC WARFARE

There's a war on.

As a matter of fact, there are a lot of wars going on at this very minute.

There have been nearly 100 since World War Two.

But there is one war which has been going on ever since there have been people on earth. The war between good and evil, between God and Satan.

And before you write that off as old-fashioned rubbish, pause and think.

● Why is it that you find it harder to build good habits than bad ones?
● Why is it that children never need to be *taught* to lie and hate and rebel?
● Why is it that the greatest wars in this century have broken out between the best educated, most advanced societies with the best standards of living?

● Why is it that moral standards are dropping, crime is rising, corruption is spreading?

Because there is a war on.

War on three fronts

Part of our problem is other people. Their influence drags us down. We are reluctant to stand up for what we know is right, and be different. The Bible

calls this powerful pressure *the world*.

Part of our problem is ourselves. There seems to be a traitor in the camp. We see what is right; we approve of it; but we often do the opposite. The Bible calls this inner weakness *the flesh*.

And part of our trouble is the Great Outside Hindrance, or Satan. Not some fun figure with cloven hooves and a forked tail. But one of God's creatures; an angel who rebelled against God and wants to involve the whole world in his rebellion. The Bible calls this evil spirit *the devil*.

That is why we find it so hard even to live up to our own indifferent standards. There is a great spiritual force of evil seducing us away from the right path, and he uses the pressures of society and our own inner weakness to drag us down.

The world…the flesh…the devil …all these oppose us.

Nobody can prove that this account of the world is true. But it is certainly what the Bible teaches. And it does make sense. It ties up with our experience of life.

In Northern Ireland there has been a war on for years. It never seems to get any better. But if you go to Ireland you will very seldom see actual street warfare.

Generally all seems peaceful and friendly. Life goes on as usual. But there is a war on all the same.

Hidden agents wait the right moment to strike. Innocent people are involved in the disasters. Attack comes when you least expect it. There is a war on.

Equally certainly there is a spiritual war going on beneath the surface of life. Hence the disease, the hate, the wars, the sins of individuals and society. And God cares.

He cares so much that he came to our world to do something about the sorry mess. If you want it summed up in a single sentence, the Bible puts it like this:

'The reason the Son of God came was to destroy the works of the devil.'

AN ASTOUNDING CLAIM

To talk about Jesus as the Son of God begs the question. Who was he? Was he the Son of God? Lots of people make claims. They need checking out. Do they match up in experience?

Evel Knievel is the highest paid entertainer in the world. He specializes in promising to do the most sensational things. And he has broken almost every bone in his body failing to keep all his promises.

He had a great idea in 1974. He was going to jump the Snake Canyon on a rocket-assisted motorcycle. It is some 1600ft wide, and the rocket would launch a parachute with him attached. He would make 30 million dollars through television and tickets. It would be an amazing spectacular.

The trouble was he did not make good his claims. His rocket fired, his parachute opened, but he only got as far as the floor of the Canyon.

Promises

The difference with Jesus was just this. He did make good his claims, all along the line.

● *He claimed to have the power to heal sick people at will — and he proved it by total success in every type of healing.*

● *He claimed to have the power to forgive sins — something only God can do. 'Your sins are forgiven you' he said to a paralyzed man — and proved his authority by healing him.*

● *He claimed to be the only one who could reveal God to men and bring men to God — and he has been doing it ever since.*

● *He claimed that he and his Father were one, and that he was the way, the truth and the life for men. He made good this claim by the quality of life he lived.*

● *He claimed to be the long-awaited Suffering Servant of God, who would take away the sins of the world — and he proved it dying on the cross.*

● *He claimed that it would be proper for men to worship him — and Thomas, his once sceptical disciple, fell down at his feet confessing 'My Lord and my God.'*

● *He claimed that he would one day be entrusted with the judgement of every man, woman and child in the universe, and that their destiny for all eternity would be determined by their relation to himself — and one day we will discover for ourselves whether that claim is true or not.*

● *He claimed that he would be put to death on a cross and rise to life again on the third day. It happened, and that is one of the strongest reasons why we can believe he really is the Son of God.*

The apostle Paul wrote to the Romans: 'Jesus was descended from David physically. But he was shown to be the Son of God by the resurrection from the dead.'

FOLLOW ME!

It is one thing to like mountains. Or read books about them. Or admire them. It is quite another thing to climb them, even roped to an expert.

If you are going to try to climb a mountain like the Eiger, you must

● trust your guide completely,
● listen to his commands and obey them at once,
● be roped to him and to others on the climb.

There is no other way you can hope to reach the top...

This is the sort of relationship Jesus Christ expects of his disciples. He did not advise people to listen to his teaching. He commanded them to follow him.

● 'Passing by the Sea of Galilee, Jesus saw Simon and Andrew casting a net into the sea (for they were fishermen). And he said to them, "Follow me".'
● 'And Jesus, looking on the young man, loved him, and said to him, "Go, sell what you have; and come, follow me".'

The good life?

This is just where the teaching of Jesus is so different from the other great teachers of the world. They all pointed to some side of the truth and said 'Follow that'. He claimed to *be* the truth and said 'Follow me'.

Others before him had taught about living a good life. Jesus claimed that he *was* God's life come among men. It made sense to invite people to share that life. How? By coming to follow him.

Many religious teachers had concerned themselves with the way to God. The difference with Jesus was that he claimed to *be* that way to God. No one could discover God as Father except through him. No wonder he invited them to follow him.

'I am the way, the truth, the life,' he said. 'No one comes to the Father except through me.' That is why he told people that they must follow him.

It is hardly surprising that these claims made him a threat to the Jewish leaders. This man was different...

The Way

Christians, as they were later called, liked to call themselves followers of the Way. They had a personal link of allegiance to Jesus.

It is important to be clear about this, for all sorts of people think they are Christians who would not say they had any personal link with Jesus Christ. They say

● I live a decent life.
● I agree with the teaching of Jesus
● I go to church

But that does not make a person a Christian. Jesus calls each of us personally to follow him.

A CHANGE OF DIRECTION

At the heart of the teaching of Jesus is the challenge to change the whole direction of our lives. This seems very strange to us these days. It does not really matter which route you choose ... they all take you to the top of the mountain.

Jesus says that they do not.

I once came across this remarkable signpost in the heart of rural Wales. One finger reads 'Llanwrthwl 4½', and the other, directly opposite, reads precisely the same. It does not matter which way you go. You land up at Llanwrthwl.

But you do not land up in the family of God by heading off in any direction you please. That is the sure way to go astray.

According to Jesus you need to *repent* and *believe*.

Repentance

Repentance does not mean shedding crocodile tears over past failures. To repent means:

- to change your attitudes to God, to what is wrong, to other people.
- to allow God to make changes in your life that are overdue but which you never got round to.
- to stop putting yourself first, and start putting God first.

God's call for repentance is nothing short of a take-over bid. It tells us that there is one way to God. Jesus is that one way. And to follow him means turning away from other paths and committing yourself to his.

Repentance was one requirement which Jesus never tired of stressing. There was one other.

Faith

- Faith does not mean believing what you know is not true.
- Faith does not mean the last resort when things are black.
- Faith does not mean agreeing with something in your mind while it makes no difference whatever to your life.

Faith means believing about somebody in such a way that you believe in them. If you are a trapeze artist, you believe that the other trapeze artist is reliable. You believe he can take your weight.

By itself, of course, that does not move you one inch from the safety of your bar.

But it does give you good grounds for committing yourself to that leap through the air which results in a very sharp change of direction.

When you do that, you show that you really believe in the other person. You quite literally bet your life on his reliability. You entrust your whole self and your future to him.

That is what the Bible means by faith. It is not blind. Jesus Christ is every bit as reliable as the trapeze artist — far more so, in fact. But I do not actually believe in him in the full sense he was calling for, until I leave the security of my perch, whatever it happens to be, and bet my whole life on his faithfulness.

Some people have called this the leap of faith. That is what it is. But it is not blind faith. It is an act of commitment, leading to a life of relationship.

Repentance and faith make that change of direction without which it is impossible to follow Jesus.

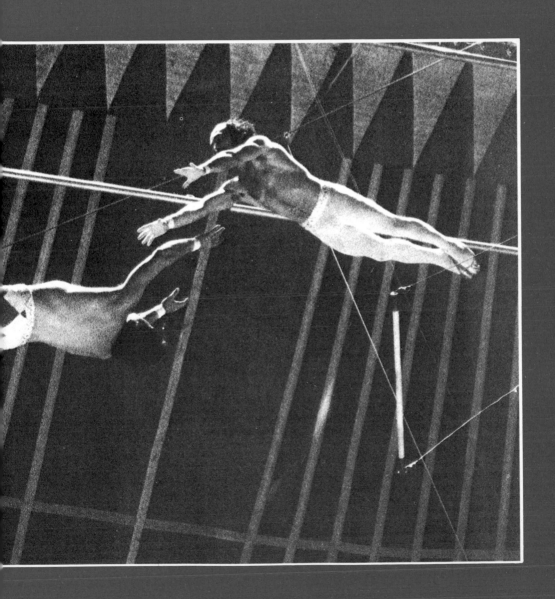

FREEDOM TO FIND YOURSELF

Iranian students wore masks to hide their identity when they demonstrated against the late Shah. We all wear masks.

There is the mask of the business man, the glamour girl, the soldier, the diplomat. We know what exterior to expect from each of them.

The smooth smile of the society hostess; the quick joke of the comedian, the cool apology of the tradesman, the bland calm of the clergyman—masks, all of them.

And inside?

Unmasked

One of the marvellous things that Jesus Christ did for everyone who came to follow him was to remove their masks. He insisted that they did not need to wear them any more. There was no reason to go on pretending.

For God himself had declared them accepted.

Once people realize that, once they come to feel it deep inside them, it brings the most profound liberation.

At last they are free to find themselves...and be themselves. Every movement worthy of the name offers freedom these days. It is a very fashionable word. Yet it is obvious that much of the freedom is in fact a new bondage. We tend to exchange one set of rules, one set of masters for another. We are still in bondage.

What of the freedom Jesus Christ offers?

Quite simply, it is the freedom to be the self that God intended us to be when he made us. That freedom has got spoiled by a variety of forces, but most profoundly of all by the sin which has put shackles on all our lives.

'Not me!' you say? That is just what the Jews said when Jesus first declared his offer of freedom. They were still wearing masks, still playing games. And gently Jesus removed the mask, and told them:

'Whoever does wrong becomes the slave of wrong.'

That is true, and depressing. That is why we wear masks to shut the unwelcome fact away.

But Jesus continued:

'If God's Son shall set you free. you will be really free.'

That is true, too. And wonderfully liberating. Set free at last from the inner grip of constant failure. Released at last to be myself. I no longer need to pretend. God has seen the worst about me and still declares me accepted. Why need I pretend to others that I am any different from what I am?

Free to be myself

● *Christian freedom liberates a person from the crippling sense of guilt. God has dealt with all that through Jesus Christ and his death.*

● *Christian freedom liberates a person from being dominated by what 'they' think or expect. He is free to be himself, the self God made him to be.*

● *Christian freedom sets a person free from constant defeat by bad habits and inadequacies. Released by the Son of God, we begin to taste real moral freedom.*

● *Christian freedom means we can be honest with each other about our failures, knowing not only that others have them too, but that God accepts us despite them.*

● *Christian freedom liberates us from bondage to a set of rules, be they new ones or old. It is the freedom to please a living person— Jesus Christ. That aim begins to dominate our motives and change our lives.*

Many Christians never realize the freedom that is their birthright. But others progressively do. And all may. For the offer of Jesus Christ stands:

'If God's Son shall set you free, you will be really free.'

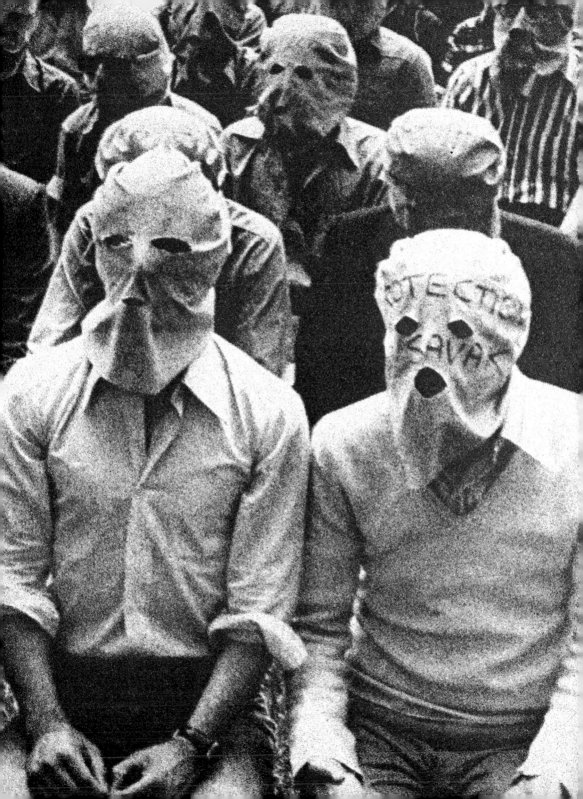

A DEATH THAT ACHIEVED EVERYTHING

One of the most amazing things about Jesus Christ is that his death is even more important than his life. In most biographies a person's death is alluded to briefly in the last chapter. In the Gospels the death of Jesus is central. Nearly half of what is written in the Gospels relates to it in one way or another.

Why?

The cross is the mark of Christianity. You find it around people's necks. You find it in their churches. Not a book—to remind you of Christ's Sermon on the Mount, say—but a cross to remind you of Christ's terrible death.

Why?

● His death was a martyr's death: Jesus was hounded to crucifixion for the sake of the unpalatable truth he taught—like lots of others down history.

● His death was a sacrificial death: he went to it willingly, making the supreme sacrifice—like lots of others down history.

But what made Jesus' death special? Quite simply, the fact of who he was. Look back to the page on 'An astounding claim'. This was no mere dying. This was God in our midst.

That is what makes the death of Jesus so special.

And here is what it tells us about God:

● **He cares about us.** Sometimes people say, 'Why does God seem so far away?' He may seem it, but he isn't. He came to our world, lived our human life and died as we must die—but in agony far worse than most of us have to undergo. God cares about us. He is not that vague 'Something' which started the world off and then left us to get on with it. He cares so much that he came. He cares so much that he died.

● **He understands our suffering.** Sometimes people say 'Why does God allow it?' Or 'Why doesn't God do something about the suffering in the world?' He has!

Nobody can give a full explanation of the pain and suffering that spoils our world and our lives. The Bible teaches that it is somehow linked with human disobedience. We have gone off God's track, and inevitably there is chaos, painful chaos, as a result.

But Christianity gives a more satisfactory account of suffering than you can find anywhere else.

Stoicism says 'Grin and bear it'.

Buddhism says 'It is all an illusion.'

Hinduism says 'It will give you a

better reincarnation.'

Christianity says 'God has not explained it fully. But he has come to share it.'

Isn't that what we want when we are suffering in hospital? Not a long lecture on the causes of our pain, but someone to come alongside, and take our hand? The cross shows that God is like that. He is the suffering God. He understands human suffering — from the inside.

● **He paid our debts.** This is the deepest thing that the cross of Christ shows us. When Jesus died, he cried out 'Finished' or 'The debt is paid'. It is as if all our wrong thoughts and words and deeds, all the flaws in our character, were one gigantic bill which we owed to the perfect, holy, loving God. He was so holy that he could not pretend it did not matter. He was so loving that he could not let it cut us off from him for ever.

So he acted. He allowed our guilt to crush him on the cross. He took our sin down into death.

'He bore our sins in his own body.'
'He has once and for all suffered for sins, the good for the bad, to bring us to God.'
'He has cancelled the account which stood accusingly against us with its legal demands. This he set aside, nailing it to the cross.'

In ways like this the New Testament writers wrestle to explain what Jesus achieved when he died on the cross.

Because he, the Eternal, paid that debt, it need never be repeated.

Because he, the innocent one, took our filthy guilt upon himself, anyone who puts his trust in him is accepted by God — free from sin.

Because he took responsibility in his death for the sins of the whole world, his cross divides people. It is both an assurance and a threat.

● It is an *assurance* if we turn to him, acknowledging our faults and recognizing that he has put them away for ever: we can be, as the New Testament puts it, 'acquitted' — forgiven for all our sin.
● It is a *threat* if we decline to turn to him, assuming we are all right as we are. The cross says we are not all right, and that it cost the Lord the agonies of a cruel death to put us in the right with him.

That's why the cross takes us to the heart of Christianity.

It is the death that achieved everything.

NEW LIFE, NEW POWER

The cross of Jesus was not the end of him.

If it had been, we could have been excused for thinking that God did not care.

If it had been, we could rightly have supposed that suffering has no purpose.

If it had been, we could rightly suppose that 'Finished' was the cry of defeat, not of victory. And we would certainly have no assurance of forgiveness.

But the whole New Testament resounds with the echoes of the resurrection of Jesus Christ. The resurrection started the Christian movement off, changing a bunch of terrified men into a task force. The resurrection spelt power, the power of God in our world. It was something utterly new.

But did it happen?

● Yes, it happened. Jesus was well and truly dead, certified as such by the Roman governor and the man in charge of the execution squad. Yet he rose.

● Yes, it happened. The tomb was empty on the third day. Just the grave-clothes were left as they had been, wrapped round the body. Like the chrysalis case when the butterfly has emerged.

● Yes, it happened. His enemies could not deny it. His followers were ecstatic about it. And they spread like wildfire.

● Yes, it happened. He kept appearing to different people in different situations for six weeks, assuring them he was alive and commissioning them to go and tell the good news all over the world.

● Yes, it happened all right. You could not explain the change in the day of worship from Saturday to Sunday if it had not. You could not explain the rise of the Christian movement if it had not. You could not explain its power to change lives if it had not.

Power to change lives. That's what the resurrection means. In our generation we have seen an utterly new dimension to power. Power to launch rockets to the moon and the stars. Undreamed of new power. But nothing compared with the power of the resurrection, which unlocked the gates of death — fast shut since the death of the first man.

What kind of power?

We don't like the idea of power too much. We remember that all power tends to corrupt. We dislike the overtones of power over other people.

But the power of the risen Christ is quite different from that.

● It is the power to go straight.

I think of the alcoholic, the compulsive gambler, the dishonest businessman — utterly changed once they come in touch with the power of the risen Christ.

● It is the power to unite in love.

I think of places where Jews and Arabs, folk from Northern and Southern Ireland, from the Black and White communities in South Africa, now live not in hatred but in love and mutual service. It is only the power of Jesus Christ, risen from the dead, which can achieve that miracle.

● It is the power to endure hardship,

opposition and brainwashing, as has been shown by the survival and growth of the church in Russia and China despite every determination by the authorities to crush them.

● It is the power to face death with triumph.

More Christians have been martyred in this generation than in any previous one. And they have gone to their deaths with calm, and with hymns of praise. They know that not even death can sever them from the living Christ.

● It is the power to change society.

Education, medicine, liberation throughout the world have been brought about more by the gospel of the risen Christ than by any other agency.

This power is not, I repeat *not*, Christians trying to be good!

The hang glider doesn't try to fly and conquer the downward pull of gravity. He simply trusts himself to a power far greater than his own: the power of the air currents to give him lift.

That is what the Christian does. He entrusts himself to the power of the risen Christ, and in that power he rises to heights he could never otherwise have reached. He has found a new life with Christ. And that life means a new power.

Jesus was a Jew.

When you see prosperous Jews in New York...

When you see inventive Jews in Israel...

When you hear of persecuted Jews in Hitler's gas chambers, or Siberian prisons...

...you are being confronted by one of God's great marvels.

● A people sprung from one man who believed and obeyed God—Abraham.

● A people 4,000 years old.

● A people who have retained their national identity throughout nearly 3,000 years of dispersion over the face of the globe.

● A people who have had no national home, no fatherland, between AD 135 when they were kicked out of Palestine and 1948 when they secured a partial return.

The people into which Jesus was born.

God's chosen people, Israel.

Chosen people

In these days of equality, words like 'chosen people' make us angry. But there is no need for us to feel like that.

God did not choose Israel because they were better than anyone else. He did not choose them because they had done something to deserve it. Nor was there any favouritism about it. He chose them for a purpose. Just as a golfer might choose a club, or a pilot choose a plane.

It was like this.

God made a world that was perfect in every way. People were perfect too. And that perfection included their relationship with God. Men and women enjoyed God's love and shared their lives with him.

But very early in the story, people chose the selfish way, and turned their backs on God. They have been doing

so ever since. So God, being the loving God he is, set out on a rescue operation.

He determined to find at least one person who would trust him in the dark—obey him to the full.

He found Abraham.

And Abraham and his wife Sarah learnt to trust God, even when all seemed black. They learnt to obey him, even when they didn't want to. They were the pioneers in the life of discipleship.

They had a son, Isaac, who had a son, Jacob.

And Jacob had twelve children.

These twelve children became the patriarchs from whom the twelve tribes of Israel were descended.

World purpose

Their story is the story of the Old Testament. It is a story of failure and success, of disobedience and faith, of commoners and kings, shepherds and prophets. It is a story of the gradual conviction becoming central to Israel's faith that there is one God alone in all the world, that they were his people bound to him by a sacred agreement and pledged to loyalty and obedience.

● They were very clear that God had chosen and commissioned them, and that this made them a special people among the nations.

● They were not so clear why. They were reluctant to see themselves as the bearers of God's truth to heathen nations. They tended to be a bit exclusive.

● But God had chosen them for a purpose—that they would provide a base for his worldwide rescue operation. Through the people of Israel he would one day spread the knowledge of himself through the entire globe.

'I am the Lord, I have called you in righteousness.
I have given you as a covenant to the people, a light to the nations.'

SALVATION THROUGH SACRIFICE

Within three generations of Abraham, within three generations of becoming a people, Israel found themselves in a terrible situation. In some ways it is curiously modern. They were embroiled with Egypt.

Abraham's grandson, Jacob (or Israel, as he was also called) went to live in Egypt during a severe famine at the invitation of his own son Joseph, who had become, by an amazing series of adventures, second-in-command to Pharaoh. But another Pharaoh arose who did not take at all kindly to the fast-increasing children of Israel within his borders, and made them serfs for his building programmes.

Egypt that had seemed the land of plenty turned out to be the land of bondage and of death.

Passover

Under the leadership of Moses, God brought about a wonderful rescue from Egypt. The children of Israel crossed the Red Sea and many of the Egyptian army were drowned when they tried to follow them.

But this whole exodus was made possible by the death of a lamb.

God made it clear to Moses that he was going to pass in judgement over the land of Egypt, and unless there was blood from a lamb on the lintel of a house, the eldest child in that house would die. So the Israelites celebrated the first Passover (which of course Jews keep to this day). Each household sacrificed a lamb. Its blood was painted up on the doorposts of the house, and they ate its flesh standing, ready for the great escape.

God was teaching his people a most important lesson:

Rescue is costly, very costly.

He is a holy God who cannot bear wickedness in his people. And when he comes in judgement, the guilty must die unless they rest under the blood of an innocent victim dying in their place.

Sin-bearer

That was a lesson which burnt itself deeply into the people. Once they had come out of Egypt, and had entered the promised land, two great factors came to dominate their personal, social and national life.

● One was the law of God, originally given through Moses, which regulated almost every aspect of life, and showed how God intended them to live.

● The other was the sacrificial system. Every morning and every evening there were sacrifices in the Temple at Jerusalem. Every Day of Atonement there was a great sacrifice involving the whole nation. Sin was confessed, and the people's guilt was passed on to a victim—normally a lamb or goat—by the high priest laying his hands on its head.

You could say that all this shedding of blood through sacrifices was a revolting waste. So it would have been, had it not pointed forward to something much greater. It was God's powerful way of teaching his people that his holiness simply cannot co-exist with evil. Death—separation from God—*has* to follow sin.

But the Old Testament was at pains to teach Israel that God has provided a way of escape. That way was to be by the death of none other than his own Son, Jesus Christ. It was paid in full, on the cross. And it was to this that the sacrificial system and the Passover looked forward.

Rescue comes through sacrifice, and by no other way.

That is the lesson Israel learnt during the twenty centuries before the coming of Christ.

There is a remarkable forward look in the religion of Israel.

• They had been rescued from Egypt, but they were always looking for a more profound liberation.

• They had a king, but he kept disappointing, and they looked for a kingdom that could not be shaken.

• They had a system of animal sacrifices, but they knew in their hearts that the blood of goats and lambs could never take away sins.

They looked forward…

Prophecy was an outstanding feature among the Jews. God would raise up men to speak his will to the people, and also to lift their hearts to what God was going to do in the future.

The New Deal

It is not surprising, therefore, that when we come to Jesus we find him fulfilling so many forward pointers, or prophecies, of the Old Testament.

• The prophets had spoken of the New Deal or New Covenant which would replace the old agreement between God and Israel which the people broke time and again. Jesus said he would inaugurate this New Deal by shedding his own blood on the cross, and he gave his followers the Holy Communion to imprint the memory of his sacrifice on the minds of every generation.

• The prophets had spoken of a king who would sit on King David's throne and reign in righteousness, and whose kingdom would be without frontiers. Jesus came announcing the arrival of that kingdom, and it has been growing ever since, so that now it literally spans the whole world.

• The prophets had spoken of the day when God would send his perfect servant to Israel, who would carry out his will in every detail, and gladly bear all the suffering involved. That famous verse, immortalized in Handel's *The Messiah*, refers to this suffering servant.

'All we like sheep have gone astray. We have turned every one to his own way. And the Lord has laid on him (the suffering servant) the iniquity of us all.'

Jesus promised to fulfil that destiny of the suffering servant of God. And he did — on the cross. This is how his friend and follower Peter described the fulfilment of that old prophecy.

'He bore our sins in his own body on the tree (the cross).'
'He has once and for all suffered for sins…to bring us to God.'

The Liberator

The Boat People, refugees from Vietnam, know the terrible bondage they are in. They know there is a better country, where freedom and justice are to be found. They are waiting, longing for that day of liberation.

And in the days of Herod, petty King of Judea, the Liberator was born. Not at all as they expected, with trumpets and armies and political success. That is not God's way. He chose a village girl to be the mother of his Liberator. He chose a stable, not a palace. And Jesus worked as a carpenter, not a prince. But he went on to teach as no man ever taught. And he went on to die as a ransom for many.

In that death he proved he was no political Liberator, wheeling and dealing for the success of his programme. To the Jews, death meant failure; worse, death on a cross meant the curse of God.

But if he bore the curse of God, it was our curse, borne so that we should never have to bear it. And out of 'political failure' came spiritual freedom for millions.

Such is the Liberator Israel longed for. And so does the rest of humanity.

A LIBERATOR

THE BURNING MEN

All the preparation for the coming of Jesus took place in the Jewish nation. Jesus lived, taught, died and rose again, all within the Jewish homeland. So when did Christianity break out from its Jewish limits and become a gospel for the whole world?

Pentecost is one of the great Jewish festivals. On that day, seven weeks after Jesus rose from the grave, people from many nations had come to Jerusalem for the celebrations. The followers of Jesus were a small, frightened group in hiding.

'Suddenly there was a noise from the sky which sounded like a strong wind blowing...then they saw what looked like tongues of fire which spread out and touched each person there. They were all filled with the Holy Spirit.'
A large international crowd gathered, and '...they were all excited, because each one of them heard the believers speaking in his own language.'

The result of these remarkable happenings was that 3,000 people came to believe in Jesus as the Messiah risen from the grave. And the Christian church as an international community was born.

All this sprang from the believers being 'filled with the Holy Spirit'.

Who is the Holy Spirit?
● The Holy Spirit is God's unseen but personal power. The Spirit led the ancient prophets to prophesy. The Spirit guided the kings of Israel and famous people in Old Testament days. But he was not for the likes of you and me.
● There are hints in the Old Testament that one day all this will change. God will send his great deliverer and 'The Spirit of the Lord shall rest upon him'.
● That is what happened with Jesus. He was able to fulfil the ancient prophecy:

'The Spirit of the Lord is upon me, because the Lord has anointed me to bring good tidings to the afflicted, to bind up the brokenhearted, to proclaim liberty to the captives and the opening of prison to those who are bound.'

He was the only person who had ever been permanently filled by God's Holy Spirit. And so he was uniquely qualified to pass that Spirit on to others.
● Things were now very different from Old Testament days. The Holy Spirit was personalized—Jesus in Spirit form. And he was permanently available—for any who would have him.

'Better if I go'
On the night before he died, Jesus said something that surprised his disciples:

'It is better for you that I go away, because if I do not go, the Helper will not come to you.'

They could not understand this and were very sad.

But he was right.

While he was confined to one human body, he could only relate to a few of them at any one time and in any one place. But once set free from the limitations of a human body, he could relate to any men, anywhere, at any time. That was much better.

So that is why the physical presence of Jesus was removed from this earth. Instead he sent his 'other self', his Holy Spirit.

When Jesus Christ was raised from the grave, it showed conclusively that death could not remove him from the world. He is alive continually, and can be known by people in all ages.

Through the Holy Spirit his wonderful presence is with everyone who believes in him.

This is why those believers we read of in the Acts of the Apostles were such burning men. They set the world on fire, and changed the course of history—not by their own brilliance, but by the power of God's Holy Spirit.

A BOOK TO LIVE BY

They called themselves 'followers of the Way'. ('Christians' was a nickname others gave them.) And the followers of the Way were notable for their map.

Christians have always been people of the book. That book is of course the Bible. The early believers had only the Old Testament, but they prized it greatly. It was the story of how God had rescued a people and prepared them for himself. More, it contained God's Word, his message to his people. It embodied God's law. Supremely, it pointed forward to God's Son.

Like all Jews, the first Christians were clear that God had revealed himself in that book. They were clear that Jesus was the climax and crown of the gradual unfolding of God's revelation in the Old Testament. So wherever they went they used the Old Testament writings to explain who Jesus was and what he had achieved.

The Old Testament was the root, and Jesus was the fruit, of God's plan to reveal himself to men.

Old and New

Very soon the earliest missionaries were carrying with them copies of the words of Jesus, and the stories of his wonderful life, death and resurrection. Naturally these began to be set alongside the sacred books of the Old Testament. And so did the writings of his closest followers. He had called them apostles—'men with mission'—and their task was to draw out for future generations the meaning of his teaching, his life, his death.

Within a comparatively short time the Gospels and letters of the New Testament had been combined with the Old Testament as the book for believers. As Augustine put it, 'the Christ who is concealed in the Old Testament is revealed in the New'.

They were people of the book.

But there was nothing rigid about this. They did not treat the Bible like the rule book of some trades union. It was a living book.

The map

That is how Christians see the Bible.

- It is not merely superb literature.
- It is not merely a source book for Christian beliefs.
- It is not a lucky dip where any verse can be squeezed to fit any situation.

The Bible is a map.

- It is a guide for the Christian community as they travel through this life.
- It is a library, full of poetry, history, letters and the like.
- It is designed by God to give us enough information to live a joyful, useful, upright and loving life in this world. It is a map, with guidelines, warnings, examples, teaching, encouragement.

But it is no flat, two-dimensional chart. It is more like that living, moving map the helicopter pilot has to fly by. Because through the Bible the living God speaks to those who are prepared to listen humbly and obey what they hear. That example to follow, that warning to heed, that promise to encourage, suddenly springs from the page and speaks to us personally. That is why Christians read it . . . privately . . . in church . . . in group study. It is a book to live by. Through it, the risen Lord gives direction to his people.

A WORLDWID COMMUNITY

'Go into all the world and make disciples of every nation.'

'You shall receive power when the Holy Spirit has come upon you, and you shall be my witnesses in Jerusalem ...and in all Judea ...and in Samaria ... and to the end of the earth.'

That is what Jesus had told his followers.

And that is precisely what they did.

In the first three hundred years the Christian faith spread throughout the Roman world, based round the Mediterranean Sea. It reached North Africa, Spain, Germany, France, Yugoslavia, Greece and Turkey.

Different nations: same family

In the nineteenth century the Christian faith spread literally throughout the world. You will find Christian communities everywhere from the tribes in the Sahara to the Eskimos near the North Pole.

The church has many different customs in different lands, and widely different forms of organization. But you will always recognize Christians, if they are being true to their Lord and to their calling.

● They share a common faith despite differences of detail: 'one body, one Spirit, one hope, one Lord, one faith, one baptism, one God and Father of us all.'

● They share a common meal—the Lord's supper, or Eucharist—in which they remember Jesus' death, draw on the strength of his risen life, and anticipate heaven.

● They keep a special day—Sunday, the day on which Jesus rose from the

dead. This is a day for rest and worship and re-creation.

Or you could look at it another way. Wherever you find the church loyal to Jesus:

● It will proclaim the teaching and challenge of Jesus.

● It will try to continue the healing ministry of Jesus.

● It will be prepared to share the suffering of Jesus, whether by mockery or by active persecution.

● It will embody something of the joy and power of Jesus.

Company on the road

Of course, the church is made up of sinful, fallible mortals...just like us.

So it is not surprising that it makes big mistakes, and at times is very unlike its Master. It does not reckon to have arrived. It is a company on the road.

But in this company you will find guilty people who have found forgiveness through the death of Jesus; lonely people who have discovered the companionship of Jesus; weak people nerved by the power of Jesus' resurrection; fearful people whom his love has made bold. You will find lives in process of change. And you will find a desire to share with others the good news of a Liberator.

Heresy has not entirely ruined them. Apathy has not entirely shrunk them (only in western Europe is there a decline). Persecution has not wiped them out. They continue, and grow, and praise God.

The church is a worldwide community, bringing the love of God to every nation.

A SECULAR SOCIETY?

And what of the world in which Christianity is so widely spread? It is a very different society from the Christian community. It has different assumptions, different goals, different standards.

In the West, society is largely secular. It has come to assume that there is no God, that man came from nothing and is going nowhere beyond himself. There is no life after death.

Though not spelt out as baldly as that, such is in fact the basic outlook of most people in secular western society.

Does it really make any practical difference if the secularists are right, and God is just a cosy dream? The answer lies in the directions society is taking.

● It makes a great difference to how we live. If there is no God who has given us rules to live by, why should we not steal—provided we are not found out?

● It makes a great difference to our attitude to life. If life is not a gift from God, there is no ultimate argument against euthanasia, abortion, murder and genocide. There is no basic reason why we should not let the hungry starve.

● It makes a great difference to the question of meaning and purpose in our lives. If we were not created to know God and enjoy him for ever but are simply the products of biological accident, then there is no good looking for purpose in life. There is none.

● It makes a great difference to our attitude to death. These days death has replaced sex as the subject you never mention. This is hardly surprising if death brings the final extinction of the meaningless ego I call 'myself'.

● It makes a great difference to marriage. So long as marriage was seen as a threesome between the partners and the Lord who invented it, there was good reason for couples to stay together. Now there seems to be neither reason nor ability. In some countries one in every two marriages collapses, with appalling results for the partners, the children and the integration of society.

● It makes a great difference to our attitude to possessions. Jesus warned people against covetousness. He said, 'A man's life does not consist in the multitude of his possessions.' Secular society is convinced that a man's life *does* consist in just that. And so covetousness becomes a way of life.

Christmas is the time when we celebrate God's free gift. But it has become so commercialized that 'grab' has replaced 'give'. Do we want a world where material or where spiritual values count for most?

As a society, we get what we really want...

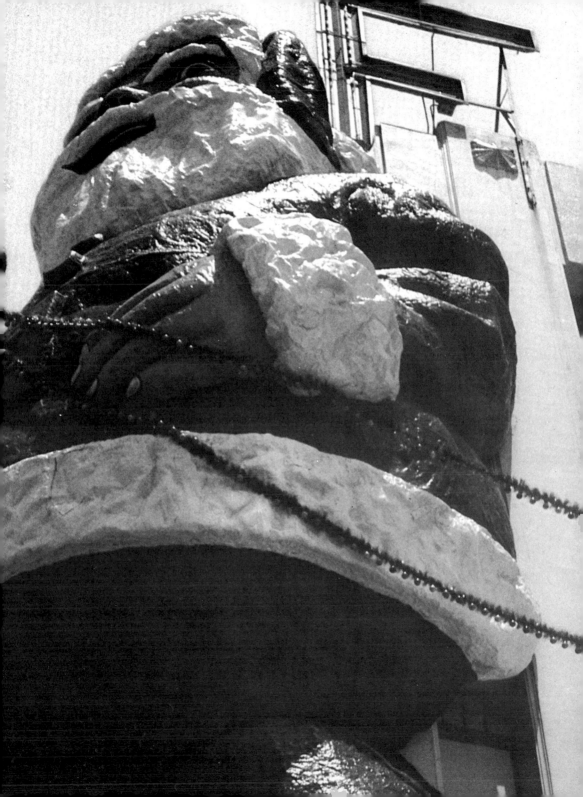

A FAITH EXPLOSION

Drop a stone in a pond, and you will not only disturb the placid surface of the water, you will send ever-widening ripples right across the pond.

That is what happened when the Holy Spirit of Jesus came into the lives of the first disciples on the Day of Pentecost, just 50 days after his resurrection.

It certainly disturbed the placid waters of Judaism. The services were droning on in the Temple as usual. Then suddenly these men were so filled with God's Spirit that they burst out praising him ecstatically in the streets.

Their teaching of a crucified Messiah, risen and able to fill men with his Spirit, disturbed the leaders of Israel. They hoped they had put a stop to this troublesome movement.

Their healing of sick people through the Spirit of Jesus was an equally unwelcome and embarrassing sign of God's power in their lives.

So was the fact that if you put them in prison they would praise God while chained in the stocks, sing hymns at midnight, and bring the gaoler to faith and baptism!

Baptism was the sign or sacrament of the new movement. People were immersed under the water as a mark of the washing away of sins through the death of Jesus, of dying with him and rising to new life through his powerful Spirit inside them. And the evidence in their lives was there for all to see.

The volcano erupts

The movement spread like wildfire. Perhaps the nearest analogy in nature is the eruption of a volcano. Once, in the middle of the night, I saw Mount Etna in eruption. It was a fantastic sight—a tremendous glare, streams of lava, clouds of steam, and an awesome demonstration of power. It was like

that as the Christian movement spread through the nations.

It began among the Jews.

'You have crucified the Messiah (the promised Liberator)', they cried. 'But God has raised him from the dead, and we are witnesses to it.'

And not only in Jerusalem, but throughout the Jewish homeland of Judea, and even in neighbouring Samaria, men and women in their thousands put their faith in Jesus and discovered the power of his living presence.

It did not stop there. Members of the occupying Roman forces came to the same conclusion and discovered the Holy Spirit was available for them too. It was the same for complete pagan outsiders, who had looked for ages with longing respect at the religion of Israel. As we have seen on the Day of Pentecost itself, when the whole thing erupted, there were representatives from many nations visiting Jerusalem for the festival. Many of them accepted the Holy Spirit into their own lives.

Dangerous fertility

When a volcano erupts, there is not a lot you can do about it...

And wherever its lava spreads, it brings fertility in its wake. Dangerous fertility, of course—you never know when there may be another eruption! But mighty fertile all the same.

Wherever the Holy Spirit has spread down the ages and across the world, there has been a wonderful crop in his wake. A crop of love and unselfishness, of education and medicine, of prisoners liberated, evil habits broken and injustice put right.

The eruption of the Christian volcano is still going on. All over the world people are tasting its power.

WORSHIPPING GOD IN A MAN-CENTRED WORLD

Christians have made their choice. They want spiritual values to count in their lives. But the pressures of immediate needs, the call of materialism, the rush and stress are still very strong. If we want to live, as the apostle Paul put it, like 'a colony of heaven', it is essential we make time to worship.

'Be still and know that I am God.'

Stillness is essential. Worship is essential. At the heart of the stress there is a deep need to draw aside with God—'the still point at the centre of the turning world.'

● Worship is not escapism. On the contrary it recharges our batteries for living effectively in this world.

● Worship is not an optional extra for when I feel like it. However I feel I need to worship. I am commanded to worship. I cannot survive as a Christian without worship.

Reflected beauty

When something beautiful is reflected in water, sometimes the reflection is so perfect that it is very hard to be sure what is real and what is reflection.

Worship has that effect. It is being so caught up with God that when we get back to everyday life we reflect something of his calm and stillness and serenity. It makes a profound difference.

Worship literally means 'worth-ship.' We declare by what we say and do that God is worthy to have the supreme place in our lives. And so it goes much deeper than an hour in church once a week.

Christians do worship God in church with others, because we are all members of the same family. We need each other. God has made us interdependent.

'Forsake not the assembling of yourselves together,' says the New Testament.

Christians also worship God in small groups. All over the world you will find such groups meeting in homes or the open air, in universities and hospitals, in barracks and government buildings. Jesus said, 'Where two or three are gathered together in my name, I am there in the midst of them.'

Christians also worship God on their own. Alone on their knees in prayer. Alone with an open Bible. Alone among the glories of nature.

But worship goes even deeper. It involves the whole life. Our bodies and personalities, our gifts and talents, our material possessions and money—all come from God. And Christians want to offer them all back to the Giver for him to use as Jesus would if he was here today.

No wonder worship is the highest possible activity of man. It is also the most far reaching. It affects the whole of life.

Clay

So think of a potter at his wheel. Those skilled, strong hands shape the clay as he sees fit. Of course Christians are not just clay. They have wills of their own. But they want to surrender themselves freely and fully to the hands of the Potter, confident that he will mould and use them as he knows best.

That degree of surrender to God, and no less, is worship.

Life no longer pivots on ourselves —but on him.

A LIFESTYLE GOVERNED BY LOVE

Worship of God and love for fellow men—these are the two great commandments.

'You shall love the Lord your God with all your heart.'
'You shall love your neighbour as yourself.'

Such was Jesus' summary of the whole duty of man. And he based it on the Old Testament.

When people manage to live like this, it stands out in startling contrast to the selfishness and small-mindedness that are apparent everywhere else. Like a cathedral, it rises above its surroundings. It is beautiful. It is imposing. It needs no justification. A Christian life is like that.

What is love?

Christian love is easily misunderstood.

- It is not weak and soft.

- It is not romantic and emotional.

- It is nothing to do with how we feel.

Christian love is as tough and uncompromising as Jesus Christ. Christian love is as unsentimental as the cross. Christian love is as practical as feeding the hungry, clothing the naked, and bandaging the lepers. The tough early Christian adventurer, Paul, wrote:

'Love is patient and kind.
Love is not jealous or boastful.
Love is not arrogant or rude.
Love does not insist on its own way.
Love is not irritable or resentful.
Love does not rejoice at wrong, but rejoices in the right.
Love bears all things, believes all things, hopes all things, endures all things.
Love never gives up.'

God's love

We do not normally grow love like that in the garden of our lives. It is a transplant from God's garden.

'The fruit of the Spirit is love.'

Christians do not love. God loves through them.

An outstanding modern example is Mother Teresa of Calcutta. She does not naturally enjoy being with the smelly, the leprous, the dying. But she is a woman full of the love of Jesus. She loves him so much that she will do anything for him. And that love-relationship with Jesus spills over in a caring love for the destitute dying in the streets of Calcutta.

In us it will take a different form.

- But love, Christian love, always reaches out to the unlovely.

- It always seeks to give rather than to get.

- It is a torch that has been kindled in the fire of God's costly love on the cross.

Love is the greatest thing in the world.

BREAKING THROUGH TO FREEDOM

Jesus Christ saw himself as God's servant, the one described in the Old Testament who would set the captives free.

Captives of every sort.

It is not surprising, therefore, that freedom is one of the leading themes of the New Testament.

'If the Son shall set you free, you shall be free indeed.'

'Am I not free? Have I not seen Jesus our Lord?'

'For freedom Christ has set us free. Do not submit again to the yoke of slavery.'

Freedom fighters

Often Christians have failed to live up to their charter of freedom. Often the most repressive regimes have come to power in states claiming the name of Christian. But wherever men have been true to Jesus Christ and the teaching of the Bible they have been freedom fighters.

In the last century, freedom for slaves was brought by Wilberforce and a few others who had a burning Christian faith, and won the day despite fanatical opposition.

Not long afterwards, Shaftesbury's legislation produced decent working conditions for the chimney boys. The Tolpuddle Martyrs led the way for trade unions to protect the rights of workers. Both acts of liberation sprang from a living Christian faith.

Today, the fight against illiteracy all over the world is being waged more by Christians than any other group. Minds are being set free.

Others are caught in the bondage of disease, and it is Christians who are taking the lead in bringing medicine to them in the most undeveloped areas. You do not find hospitals of an atheist foundation in the really primitive areas of the world.

Liberation

Prejudice enslaves men. When Eldridge Cleaver, on the far left of American politics, and Chuck Colson, well to the right, came to faith in Christ, their prejudices against one another disappeared. Christ liberates men from prejudice.

When floods, disease and famine struck Bangladesh, Christians cared. Like Jesus they could not see men trapped in such conditions and remain unaffected. So they did not merely give money. Nurses, plumbers, doctors, builders actually went out to liberate the captives in such a situation — for the most part through Christian agencies and out of love for Jesus.

In South Africa, it is often Christians and churches who are trying to point another way than the road of segregation.

Who are the men who are protesting against Soviet tyranny from within the Soviet Union? Many of them, like Solzhenitsyn himself, are Christians.

Jesus Christ has declared himself on the side of freedom. He is the Liberator of mankind. And those who loyally follow him are champions of liberation at every level.

LIVING FOR OTHERS IN A SELFISH WORLD

As people in the West look for more sophisticated leisure activities, eating out becomes ever more resplendent. There are even re-creations of medieval banquets—no expense spared.

The contrast with the empty food bowls of the unfortunate is stark and shocking. We feel sorry for the child; we may contribute something to a charity, but then we forget. It is, after all, natural to look after our own interests.

Transfusion

The gap between the rich and the poor countries of the world is widening all the time . . . and the rich countries refuse to do anything to alter the economic arrangements that bring it about. Of course. It is natural to look after our own interests...

But Christianity is un-natural. It is supernatural. It is nothing less than the imparting of God's own love to our selfish hearts. When that transfusion takes place, it is bound to make a difference.

'Let us not love in word or in speech, but in deed and in truth,' says the apostle John. What does that love look like?

● **It makes a difference in lifestyle.** Christians will not strive to amass as much money and possessions as they can. They see all they have as belonging to God. They merely administer it. Their home, their money, their material possessions all belong to him. They seek to act accordingly. Their homes are open, their giving generous, their eating habits simple, their house and possessions unpretentious. At least, they should be...

● **It makes a difference in home life.** In many families, selfishness reigns supreme, with husbands, wives and children all doing their own thing and pressing their own rights. Christians try to take a very different stance.

Husband and wife try to outdo each other in love and self-sacrifice. . . .

The husband is out to protect his wife from worry and strain, to give himself to her in love and thoughtfulness, and to make any sacrifice for her.

The wife seeks to submit in love to her husband, to be affectionate towards him, to support him— forgetting herself and her 'rights.'

The children aim to obey and honour their parents as they would the Lord— while the parents are careful not to provoke and irritate their children with needless prohibitions.

You will find it all in Paul's letter to the Ephesians. Revolutionary stuff for family living. And the wonder is, it works!

● **It makes a difference to industrial relations.** All over the West, management and labour see each other as enemies. 'Squeeze all you can from the other side' seems to be the motto. Industrial relations are often the law of the jungle. But how about this teaching from the New Testament?

For management: 'Do the honest thing by your employees, and have done with threats. Remember, both you and they have a Master in heaven. And there is strict impartiality with him.'

For employees: 'Put your back into your work for your earthly employers. Do not skimp the job, hoping it will get by. Seek to please Christ in all you do. You are working, remember, for the Lord and not just for men.'

For the thief: 'Let him who stole steal no more, but rather let him work, doing an honest day's work so that he may have the wherewithal to give to those in need.'

Who says Christianity does not make a difference?

The love revolution is the greatest power in the world.

It only needs to be tried.

Wherever the church has been loyal to its Founder, it has been marked by love, self-sacrifice and freedom. But the church does not believe God's kingdom can be brought in by human effort. Christians work for the improvement of this world as if there were no other. But they are only strengthened to do so because there *is* another.

Death is not the end.

The Christian hope of life after death is not based on the idea that the human soul is naturally immortal. No, Christians believe that eternal life, like everything else in Christianity, is a gift from the generous God who has set us free.

'The gift of God is eternal life through Jesus Christ our Lord.'

Even if there were no life after death, I would rather be a Christian than an atheist. I am not aware that I am moved by a desire to continue existing for ever. It is enough for me to know the love and forgiveness and joy of the Lord here and now.

But he has said that he will not scrap me at death.

His people are precious to him.

Transformation

So he has devised a transformation that will take them from this life to the next. The next life will be spent with him and his people for ever in the new dimension called heaven.

The God who works in grace is the same God who works in nature. And nature gives a wonderful illustration of what life after death will be like.

The Swallowtail caterpillar is not a particularly beautiful beast. Not very mobile. Only interested in eating . . .

But the caterpillar comes to a stage when its caterpillar life must end.

CREMATORIUM

It grows disinterested in eating. It becomes restless. It spins itself a cocoon, and turns into a chrysalis. To all intents and purposes it is dead.

But really it is very far from dead. That caterpillar existence is transformed into the totally new dimension of living enjoyed by the butterfly. And the Swallowtail butterfly is extremely beautiful. It is highly mobile. It is interested in flowers and sunshine. It soars high among the trees...

Not the end

So it is with Christians after death.

Here on earth we are not very beautiful creatures, despite the grace of God at work in us. Often we are selfish, earthbound in our interests. There is something restless about us.

But when we die, that is not the end of us. We emerge into the sunshine of God's home — the same people we were on earth, only wonderfully transformed. The caterpillar has turned into a full butterfly. No longer selfish. No longer earthbound. But free to enjoy the totally new dimension of existence beyond the grave.

There is nothing materialistic about

all this. Heaven, as the Bible describes it, is not a place of sensuous delights. It is an utterly different quality of experience. Heaven is to earth what the world of the butterfly is to the world of the caterpillar.

No self-respecting caterpillar is enthusiastic about ending his days in a cocoon . . .

But no self-respecting butterfly would want to go back to being a caterpillar again. . .

'To depart and to be with Christ is far better.'

HAS THE HUMAN RACE A FUTURE?

The future exercises a great hold over us.

You need some idea of the future if you are to achieve anything in the present. The trainee soldier, businessman, athlete, politician—they all have a vision of the future. And it determines the course they take.

All the great philosophies of the day have a map of the future. The humanists look for an earth where reason and mutual consideration flourish. The Communists look for the arrival of full socialism.

Scrapheap or garden?

What does Christianity have to say about the future of mankind?

Christians do not agree with the pessimists who think that the world is going to run down or blow itself up. Nor do they agree with the optimists who think that we are improving all the time and Utopia is round the corner.

To both these common attitudes towards the future Christians respond with a 'yes' and 'no.'

● *The pessimists are right in despairing of human nature—but wrong in supposing that there is no hope. They have left God out of account.*

● *The optimists are right in believing that the destiny of our world is a garden, not a scrapheap. But they are wrong in thinking that* *man can bring it about by any social or political system. It is God who will bring it about.*

Christians hope for a great transformation, brought about by Jesus Christ. For this world has not seen the last of him. The New Testament teaches that at the end of history he will return. Then he will no longer be the despised Galilean suffering and dying for us—but the rightful king of the universe reigning over us.

The Bible writers struggle with picture language to bring home to us this hope of a transformed universe. Here is a sample from the book of Revelation:

'Then I saw a new heaven and a new earth; for the first heaven and the first earth had passed away, and the sea was no more. And I heard a loud voice from the throne saying, "Behold, the dwelling of God is with men. He will dwell with them, and they shall be his people and God himself will wipe away every tear from their eyes, and death shall be no more, neither shall there be mourning nor crying nor pain any more, for the former things have passed away."'

The return of Christ

● The return of Jesus Christ will finalize God's reign in his world.

● The return of Jesus Christ will see the abolition of evil.

● The return of Jesus Christ will see those who died in faith raised to share eternity with him.

And the whole universe, says the New Testament, waits on tiptoe for this climax of all history.

Indeed, the Bible ends like this: 'Surely I am coming soon!' says Jesus. 'Amen, come Lord Jesus!' says his church.

That is the Christian hope for the future.

And how do we know this is not a mere pipe dream—pie in the sky? Because at the centre of history God gave a first instalment of his future harvest. Jesus Christ rose from the grave to a new quality of life, resurrection life. It was a pointer to the future God has for his world.

The Christian hope for the destiny of mankind is based on the resurrection of Jesus Christ.

That is why the person who knows the risen Christ can live in hope, and work with confidence, even when all the appearances are gloomy.

He knows that even now the Lord God almighty is reigning behind the scenes of history. And one day that will become blindingly apparent.

The human race has a future. The more pressing question is, have we? And the answer lies in our response to Jesus Christ.